This book is dedicated to all who find Nature not an adversary to conquer and destroy, but a storehouse of infinite knowledge and experience linking man to all things past and present. They know conserving the natural environment is essential to our future well-being.

SEQUOIA & KINGS CANYON
THE STORY BEHIND THE SCENERY®

by William C. Tweed

William C. Tweed is a career professional of the National Park Service. Since receiving his doctorate in history from Texas Christian University, he has been involved in a wide spectrum of park-related activities. Having spent more than 25 years exploring Sequoia and Kings Canyon National Parks, Bill is intimately acquainted with these awesome Sierran parks, whose slopes encompass an incredible variety ranging from the tiniest foothill denizen to the loftiest mountaintop.

Sequoia & Kings Canyon National Parks, *located in central California, were established in 1890 to preserve giant sequoias and Mt. Whitney, the highest mountain in the lower 48 states.*

Front cover: Giant-sequoia grove, photo by Gail Bandini. Inside front cover: Forest cascade, photo by David Muench. Title page: Douglas squirrel, photo by Larry Burton. Pages 2/3: Fog-misted sequoias, photo by David Muench.

Book design by K. C. DenDooven.

Sixth Printing, 1992

On the slopes of the rugged Sierra Nevada, the giant sequoias inhabit a forest realm that they have ruled for millennia. From the mists of the ancient past they have emerged—a tribute to an incredible will to survive, and the largest of all the living things on earth.

In Sequoia and Kings Canyon—the twin national parks of the southern end of California's Sierra Nevada—spring flowers bloom from January until October; it takes that long for spring to move from the warmest foothill exposures to the coldest slopes of the highest peaks. The rise in elevation is so tremendous—from about 1,700 feet at park headquarters, Ash Mountain, to 14,495 feet on the lofty summit of Mount Whitney—that within the parks there are places where it almost never snows and places where the snows never melt. Some areas are so dry that plants must shed their leaves in midsummer and small animals must produce their own water in order to survive. Yet the parks contain living glaciers and thousands of cold, clear mountain lakes.

No one species of plant or animal can live in *all* these vastly differing areas. Each of the many macro- and micro-climates of the parks includes just those forms of life that are particularly adapted to it. Even the giant sequoias for which the parks are famous grow in only a relatively small portion of the total area of the parks. It is this *variety* that is the essence of Sequoia and Kings Canyon National Parks, a surprise to many visitors who have long held a conception of the area as only big trees, big mountains, and cool, green shade.

The difference begins to be revealed when entering the Sequoia, or southern, entrance. One finds not a welcoming forest of giant trees but a dry scrub forest of brush and oak, where few things grow more than twenty-five feet tall and summer temperatures may exceed one hundred degrees. This is the foothill zone, lying at the base of the Sierra Nevada. It is in itself a diverse and rewarding area, but its attractions are often overlooked in our eagerness to experience nature on a grander scale.

After about an hour's drive upward on the winding, twisting road, the arid heat of the foothills gives way to the inviting shade of the conifer forest, cooler by perhaps as much as twenty-five degrees. (Even the hottest summer spells may produce temperatures no higher than the eighties.) The transition is abrupt, occurring at about 5,000 feet and springing into view, quite literally, around a bend in the road.

JOSEF MUENCH

The Sierra

This is the realm of the giant sequoias, the largest living things on earth, the magnet that first drew attention to the region and caused it to be set aside as a national park over a century ago. The ancient sequoias easily dominate this world with their individuality and massiveness, but even if they were absent, this would still be a forest of giants, with its huge sugar pines and great firs.

The tight curves now give way to more gentle ones as the road approaches the upper limits of the forest, and above 7,000 feet our vehicle must be abandoned. Only foot trails lead upward from

— Land of Variety

the forest belt, and one must "take to the trail" in order to experience at close range the grandeur of the High Sierra.

At 10,000 feet, an alpine land emerges. Here, within sight of the warm foothills, temperatures seldom exceed the seventies. Snow falls in any season and may lie on the ground for nine or ten months of the year, and plants have only a few frost-free weeks in midsummer in which to renew their precarious hold on life. Trees and other vegetation are sparse and strangely stunted, effects of the prolonged, severe winters. Nearing the awe-inspiring summits of the Sierra Nevada, the land becomes so cold and harsh that most living things cannot survive at all.

Within only a few hours, we have traversed a land of infinite variety and incredible extremes to stand in the exalted region of the Sierra Crest, which bounds the parks on the east. Mount Whitney, the highest point in the contiguous United States, barely tops these great peaks, many of which exceed 14,000 feet. Beyond this formidable wall lies a vast desert, and Death Valley—but that is another world, another story.

Of Time and Mountains

Sequoia and Kings Canyon National Parks occupy only a small portion of the southern Sierra Nevada, a mountain range that in its entirety stretches some four hundred miles along the eastern boundary of California and is itself a part of the much larger mountain complex that covers most of western North America. The story of the origin of the Sierra Nevada, then, is part of a geologic story that covers an area far larger than the Sierra itself.

Through the years, many theories have been proposed to explain the existence of the obviously related mountain ranges of the West. In recent years, however, the *plate tectonics* theory has gained wide acceptance. Simply stated, it holds that the surface of this planet consists of a series of relatively rigid but ever-moving plates. In certain areas, such as the Mid-Atlantic Ridge, new surface material is even now emerging from within the earth. In other locations, plates are being pushed one under the other. The western coast of North America was once such a place. Geologists tell us that the plate that formed the floor of

GALEN ROWELL

The Spaniards named these mountains the Sierra Nevada, *"snowy mountain range." And snowy indeed they are! Portions of Sequoia and Kings Canyon National Parks receive almost three hundred inches of snow annually. In the highest parts of the Sierra, massive snowfields last late into summer.*

DAVID MUENCH

Huge, gray granite blocks contrast strikingly with fragile, vivid Sierra primroses. These ancient rocks cooled deep within the earth millions of years ago and were forced to the surface in recent geological time. The Sierra Nevada consists almost entirely of granite, which is continually exposed to the erosive action of rain, snow, and ice.

the Pacific Ocean moved northward—and hence under—the plate that formed the North American continent for a long period, ending about 25 million years ago. Since the end of this collision, a general uplift of western North America has built the modern Sierra Nevada.

The plate-tectonics theory, incidentally, also explains the granitic composition of the Sierra Nevada. This relatively light rock moved upward, in molten form, as the Pacific plate moved under North America. Later, as compression and stress continued, these hardened rocks were uplifted and then exposed through erosion. (Small areas of the parks preserve remnants of older rocks that once covered the granite. These ancient rocks are composed of badly distorted sea sediments, including sea shells and other calcium-rich materials that hardened into marble. Numerous caves have dissolved out of these calcareous formations.)

ALTITUDE AND THE WEATHER

The familiar premise that higher elevations are cooler than lower ones of the same region holds true in the Sierra Nevada. A common rule of thumb is that temperatures are reduced by about one degree (Fahrenheit) for every three-hundred-foot rise in elevation. Using this scale, and knowing that the Sierra Nevada in the vicinity of Sequoia and Kings Canyon is nearly three miles tall, the highest points in the parks are nearly fifty degrees cooler than the western base of the range. It is this dramatic but steady decrease in temperature in relation to increasing elevation that accounts for much of the diversity of life in the Sierra.

Consider another fact: Not only does it become cooler as elevation increases, it becomes wetter. The forty inches of annual precipitation

Golden eagle

received at 6,000 feet in the southern Sierra is nearly twice that of the 2,000-foot level—and more than four times that of the floor of the San Joaquin Valley to the west.

Unlike temperature, however, precipitation is not affected by elevation in direct ratio to it. Heaviest precipitation in the parks seems to occur in the 5,000- to 8,000-foot range; above this it declines, becoming fairly light on some of the highest ridges. This is easily understood given the nature of the storms that sweep this region.

Most rain and snow falls here during general storms occurring between October and May and coming from the Gulf of Alaska. Because they cross the ocean, the storms become relatively warm by the time they reach California (producing snow only in the mountain areas). The cloud masses that comprise the storms travel at relatively low altitudes, with the densest portion moving in no higher than about 8,000 feet on the western slopes. Areas lying above this level therefore receive less precipitation. (The snowpack at such elevations is greater, however, simply because the lower temperatures at these heights keep the snow from melting.) The eastern slopes, facing away from the storms, also receive less moisture.

The diversity of the Sierra Nevada—and of the 864,383 acres of Sequoia and Kings Canyon—is a result, then, of the elevational and weather differences encompassed in the three natural zones of the Sierra—foothills, forest, and high country. And it is in the plants and animals of these zones that the distinct character of each is best revealed.

The Foothills

The August sun, early and hot, floods the parched western foothills of Sequoia National Park. Three months have passed without rain, and it will be at least two more before the summer drought abates. Still, there is a touch of coolness in the air. But it will soon be gone; even before the morning shadows disappear the temperatures will be into the nineties.

Life stirs but little in the morning light. It's as if foothill occupants know the sun will soon turn the landscape into a baking furnace. The only sound is the noisy comment of a solitary scrub jay as a rattlesnake, after a long and unsuccessful night of hunting, retreats into a cool den to await the darkness.

The lacy patterns of a slender alder add color and grace to the foothill scene in springtime.

Summer in the foothills brings extremes of dryness and heat (afternoon temperatures often exceed one hundred degrees), and the hillsides turn brown. Plants that continue to function during this trying time, such as the yucca (foreground), must be highly drought-resistant. In this harsh environment, most animals choose the nighttime to pursue their various activities.

GLENN VAN NIMWEGEN

A small gray fox, more successful, descends with his kill—an unwary cottontail—through the summer-browned wild oats toward its rocky den near an almost-dry stream. Relinquishing the rabbit for a moment, he pauses to drink. Here and there, along the failing stream, survivors from the lush, green springtime that ended in May peek through. Water-loving horsetails and willows line the stream, together with broad-leaved alders and sycamores whose intense green contrasts strongly with the harsh, wheat-colored slopes of the steep banks above, where wild oats and other winter grasses prosper.

Scattered across the golden-textured slopes are stunted oak specimens—some evergreen, some deciduous, but all the same olive-green color indicative of a dry location. On the driest slopes, this oak-and-grass community is replaced by dense stands of wiry brush consisting largely of a single evergreen plant known as *chamise*. Its narrow, needle-like leaves are also olive-green, but from a distance this color is subdued by the brown of the seed stalks on the ends of the branches.

A TWO-SEASON CLIMATE

Sequoia and Kings Canyon National Parks share their climate with much of California. Two seasons predominate—one warm and dry, the other mild and wet.

The wet season usually begins in November

Springtime greens provide a luxurious prelude to the drab browns of summer and fall. Soaking winter rains allow foothill slopes to become bright meadows with occasional spectacular wildflower displays.

WILLIAM C. TWEED

Against a wheat-colored slope, a sturdy oak contrasts with the dramatic form of a manzanita, whose dark, reddish branches spread close to the ground like graceful, beckoning arms. Subtle variations in texture and color are the basis of much of the natural beauty of the foothills. Individual trees and shrubs are seldom large.

Despite their aridity, the foothills of Sequoia and Kings Canyon are continuously being shaped by flowing water. Sierran streams, such as the Kaweah River that drains the western half of Sequoia, carve ever deeper into the bedrock heart of the mountains. The great canyons of the Kings River were initially cut in this manner.

GLENN VAN NIMWEGEN

and persists into April. During these months, large-scale but usually gentle storms bring rains that last for days at a time. Temperatures are moderate, climbing from the light frosts of nighttime to the fifties or even the sixties by afternoon. Periods of heavy frost may occur, but only after the coldest storms. Total rainfall during the wet season varies greatly from year to year, but twenty inches is about average.

By April the foothills begin to warm up, and the rains diminish in both frequency and intensity. The dry season, May through October, is *indeed* dry; it produces less than ten percent of the annual rainfall, and many locales go through this period without any measurable precipitation at all.

The warming trend continues, and by late June or early July it is truly summer. Afternoon temperatures hover around the century mark—and often rise significantly above it. A "cool" spell may mean temperatures in the low nineties. Nighttime temperatures in the sixties and seventies are common.

The effects of the two-season system of the foothills are most pronounced on its inhabitants. During the latter part of the wet season, as tem-

peratures warm, conditions are ripe for rapid plant growth; even the soils of the steep hillsides are damp and fertile. Foothill plants have been preparing for this short, luxuriant period and are quick to seize opportunities for growth. Annual grasses and flowers begin to grow as soon as the soil is wet, in November or December.

By January the pervasive summer-brown of the hillsides has been replaced with a mantle of green. Wildflowers appear in increasing numbers, and by early April the open, grassy slopes are ablaze with color. Even before the flowers have gone to seed, the shrubs, too, are in bloom—first the redbud and other shrubs of the damper locations and then the chamise and other bushes of the chaparral, or brush forest.

By late May most of this activity has abruptly ceased. Grasses and flowers wither and brown; shrubs and trees move toward their summer state of at least a partial dormancy. Through evolutionary time, foothill plants have adapted to this seasonal cycle, and now they rigidly hold to the system. Even when a late, wet winter keeps soils moist beyond early May, the hillsides still go brown—right on schedule!

Like many foothill plants, the California buckeye has developed special adaptations that allow it to prosper in an arid climate. The annual cycle of the buckeye is synchronized not so much with temperature as it is with moisture: The tree leafs out in late winter, produces finger-like white flowers in May as the dry season begins, and sheds its leaves in August. The hardy chaparral (on slope beyond) is also uniquely suited to the dry environment here.

Water takes on a special beauty when it flows through dry lands. Each of the three major river systems of Sequoia and Kings Canyon is born in the high country and is fated to flow into the foothills. These cold, clear mountain streams sometimes seem incongruous in the hot foothill country, but they provide important habitats for foothill wildlife. This river, the Kaweah, flows through the town of Three Rivers and constitutes an ever-present source of visual beauty and soothing sound that almost any resident can enjoy from his own yard.

DAVID MUENCH

PLANT ADAPTATIONS

The long, dry summer season is responsible for many striking individual characteristics of foothill life. Unlike plants that live in climates where summer is the prime growing season, most annual plants of the Sierran foothills avoid the summer altogether, concentrating their growth in cooler wet periods. The few annuals that do grow here in summer, such as the tarweed, must develop narrow, water-conserving leaves and extensive root systems that search out every available pocket of water.

The lengths to which perennial shrubs and trees go in their adaptations are as extreme as the annuals. Take the California buckeye—a common, small foothill tree usually found on open, grassy slopes together with oaks and small annuals. This tree is descended from tropical ancestors accustomed to generous water supplies. The buckeye enjoys no such luxury, of course; yet it retains the broad, soft leaves of its forebears.

These leaves present a serious problem for the buckeye during summer, since their generous surfaces allow large amounts of water to evaporate.

To counteract the water loss, the resourceful buckeye has adjusted its deciduous cycles to fit the two-season nature of the foothill environment it now inhabits. It puts out its broad, green leaves in late winter, when water is readily available. It is in bud by April and in bloom by May. The blooming cycle is completed by late June, when soil moisture is exhausted, at which point the buckeye produces hard, nut-like seeds. Now the buckeye displays an adaptation that is peculiar to the foothill environment: Its leaves gradually wither and drop, so that by August only bare branches ending in seed balls remain. The tree stays in this dormant state for the next six months, returning

to life only when soil moisture is adequate to spur continuation of the cycle.

Far different are the survival strategies employed by the *chaparral*, the brushland plant community of the driest foothill slopes that is often accurately described as a "drought-dwarfed forest." The thick, wiry brush is comprised mainly of evergreen plants, which photosynthesize food throughout the wet season. Most chaparral leaves are narrow, thick, and waxy—all features that reduce moisture loss during the dry season.

Chaparral species are sun-loving. Other, more shade-tolerant species occasionally germinate and grow underneath the thick brush. This may lead to problems as the sheltered plants grow taller and surpass the chaparral itself, which seldom exceeds ten feet in height. If left unchecked, the cha-

A bobcat, nocturnal predator of the foothill country, tenses in alarm.

parral environment could be ultimately destroyed. The chaparral, however, manages to combat the challenge, with the aid of a powerful, if surprising, ally; this friend is *fire*.

The long, dry season created a situation wherein the foothill zone is highly flammable and fire is a frequent visitor. Lightning bolts from the occasional thunderstorms that drift down from the mountains may ignite the zone and cause many natural brush fires. The situation, however, is not as bad as it may seem.

The traditional belief that fire is an enemy of all plant life is untrue; it is actually *necessary* for the procreation of many species. Furthermore, some species have features that expressly *encourage* fire. In the case of the chaparral, the chemical composition of many of its woods has evolved to include a number of highly flammable substances. Most chaparral plants actually burn better when green than when dry!

This might seem rather like cutting off your nose to spite your face. But there is more to this fascinating story: The plant parts above ground are indeed consumed by fire, but most chaparral species have special root systems that fire cannot touch. As soon as the wet season begins, these roots send forth vigorous sprouts of new growth. In two or three years, the brush once again totally covers the ground, but *without* the invaders of pre-fire days!

ANIMAL ADAPTATIONS

Wildlife of the foothills has adapted to the environment in ways just as unique as those of the plants. In fact, of the three natural regions of the Sierra, the foothill zone supports the widest variety and largest number of animals—not too surprising, since this area provides abundant food and a moderate climate the year around. The warm foothills are particularly hospitable to reptiles; lizards and snakes are common. The oak-and-grass woodland is an excellent source of food for

14

ERWIN & PEGGY BAUER

Great horned owl

many small rodents, and the dense chaparral harbors a variety of bird life.

Most foothill animals are nocturnal, a result of the long dry season, when it is just too hot for daytime activity. On a late-summer afternoon drive, when air temperatures may exceed 100° (and that of exposed rocks and soil may exceed 140°), only a few birds may be seen in the open.

In contrast, the cool hours before dawn are alive with activity. Small animals such as mice and rats come out at night to feed on grasses and acorns, when they are protected by the covering darkness. It is never dark enough, however, to discourage predators; and nocturnal creatures such as the rattlesnake, bobcat, fox, coyote, raccoon, ringtail, and owl are all very much in evidence.

It is a curious fact that the true *wilderness* of Sequoia and Kings Canyon lies in the foothills, that portion closest to civilization. The grandness of the great sequoias and the magnificence of the High Sierra are powerful attractions that invite exploration by a multitude of people, but the charms of the foothills are less obvious, and so this area is rarely traversed. This situation is beneficial in that the foothills are allowed to exist in a fairly stable wilderness condition, unnoticed and thus unmolested by man. But at the same time, man is missing much that this greatly diverse area—with its unique and delightfully resourceful life forms—is offering right at his very doorstep.

ERWIN & PEGGY BAUER

The coyote is particularly well adapted to life in the foothills. The large ears and sharp eyes of this dog-like animal add to its efficiency as a hunter.

The Realm of the Giants

The August sun that floods the foothills with such ferocity is gentle as its searching rays probe the dense mass of evergreen that bands the mountains. The tree tops, towering hundreds of feet above ground, are first to catch the light, and in the cool quiet below, a small, dew-bejeweled meadow of lush grasses and bright wildflowers glistens.

A mule deer, a doe, moves out into the meadow. In the forest she had been almost invisible, her brown coloring a perfect camouflage in the shadowy, decaying world beneath the trees. But as she moves into the meadow, albeit cau-

tiously, she is a bright, warm, and very visible spot in the intense green of the grasses. A few yards more and cover is again attained, this time in grasses and flowers so tall that only the doe's alert ears give her presence away. The quiet shadows of dawn provide a time for undisturbed grazing. Soon the searching sunbeams will pierce the tree canopy above, and the dampness of the cool dawn will be dispelled for another day.

From the forest comes the agitated chirp of the chickaree, a tree squirrel, asserting his territorial rights to a trespassing blue-and-black jay. The bird moves on, and the squirrel returns to his work. Leaving his small fir tree and crossing the forest floor of decaying logs, branches, and leaves, he hops to the massive base (nearly thirty feet across) of a towering, cinnamon-colored tree.

It does not matter to the chickaree that the fibrous bark he climbs belongs to one of the oldest and largest living things on earth and that the branch he carefully selects is four feet thick, fifty feet long, and over a hundred feet off the ground! All that matters to the chickaree is the numerous small green cones he finds near the end of the branch. He works rapidly and intently, severing the cones at a rate of one per second. As they are cut, the hard cones land with gentle thuds in the thick forest carpet far below.

The mule deer, the chickaree, and the giant sequoia are all inhabitants of the great conifer forest that clothes the western slope of the Sierra Nevada. The boundaries of this immense forest are defined by climate—more specifically, the winter

KENT & DONNA DANNEN

The silhouette of a mule deer against an incense cedar evokes one of the many moods of the dense forests that clothe the Sierra.

A mist-shrouded, 2,000-year-old giant invites the friendly touch of one of the young of a much newer species.

16

storms of the Sierra. Temperatures cause these limits to vary, of course, but in the southern Sierra, 5,000 feet is the average winter snow line at the lower edge. Below this, in the foothills, most precipitation falls as rain. The broad-leaved plants that thrive there would fare poorly in the heavy snow country above, where large accumulations of ice and snow would break or split their branches.

The evergreens of the forest, however, have tall, narrow profiles and needle-like leaves; thus, they are well suited to heavy snow conditions. The conifer forest of Sequoia and Kings Canyon National Parks is, then, a *snow forest*, a community of plants and animals that have adapted specifically to a land where the snow falls heavy and lies deep.

The upper limit of the conifer forest also is defined by snow and cold. Above about 9,000 feet, colder temperatures and abrasive, blowing snow prevent forest growth. Individual trees may grow there, but dense stands are rare.

A Four-Season Cycle

Unlike the foothill zone, the forest belt of the Sierra enjoys a true four-season cycle. Spring usually arrives near the end of March, when longer days and rising temperatures finally begin to melt the snow that has been piling up since November.

In the Sierra, spring is an unpredictable and short-lived season often punctuated by late snows and cold fogs, although a few summerlike days may occur. Generally speaking, the snowpack is nearly gone by the first of June.

Summer in the forest is a gentle time. Only a few thunderstorms interrupt the prolonged dry weather of June through September. Daily temperatures fluctuate from the fifties to the seventies and almost never—at 7,000 feet—exceed the upper eighties. The mild temperatures and thick vegetation serve to prevent rapid evaporation of winter moisture. A steady drying does take place as summer passes, but even in the heat of August the meadows remain moist and many of the small forest streams continue to flow.

The transition from summer to fall is subtle. Temperatures drop gradually, and by late September the few deciduous plants of the forest begin to shed their leaves. Cooling continues throughout October, and in November heavy frosts arrive. Fall is a relatively long season, in which a few late but light storms are the only warning of the winter to come.

Sierran winters are famous for their severity in terms of heavy snows. In the forests of the southern Sierra, about two-thirds of the forty to fifty inches of precipitation received annually falls during the storms of winter. An average winter

Like all living things, each of the giant sequoias of the Sierra Nevada passes through a distinctive and predictable life cycle. It begins as a lacy, symmetrical seedling, grows rapidly to a tall, slender young adult, fills out as it matures and passes into old age, and eventually crashes back to earth in death. Here a fallen giant serves, as it often does, as the protector of new seedlings and the inspiration for young imaginations.

M. WOODBRIDGE WILLIAMS

18

"The Nation's Christmas Tree," so designated by Congress, is otherwise known as "General Grant," ancient monarch of Grant Grove, Kings Canyon. For more than half a century, at every Christmas season, holiday celebrants have staged special Christmas services at the snow-wreathed base of this towering giant.

This particular photograph, by the well-known landscape photographer Josef Muench, was selected as one of 118 pictures to be sent on each of the interstellar spacecraft Voyager 1 and Voyager 2, launched in August and September of 1977 and now traveling through space in the outer solar system. According to Carl Sagan, spokesman and chairman of the NASA Voyager Record Committee, the photo was chosen to illustrate snow ("the white substance covering the tree") to extraterrestrials and thus emphasize the presence of water on the planet Earth. The picture also indicates the great size of the sequoia tree by including human figures and demonstrates that on this planet "things live naturally where temperatures fall below freezing."

JOSEF MUENCH

Sequoia's great monolith, Moro Rock, soars high above the valley. From its summit (accessible via a safe masonry stairway), one can revel in a magnificent, untrammeled view of the Great Western Divide.

The crushing weight of snow compresses the smaller trees of a Sierra snow forest into perfect, pristine triangles.

DAVID MUENCH

Monkey flowers

WILLIAM C. TWEED

may bring 250 inches of snow, and snowpacks of five to ten feet are common. Perhaps once in a decade a truly heavy snowfall will occur. During the winter of 1969, for example, Lodgepole in Sequoia National Park received over 440 inches of snow! For the most part, however, winter temperatures are mild (at least for a mountain area), ranging from the teens to the thirties and seldom dropping below zero.

20

Plant Life in the Forest

Obviously, such conditions have a tremendous impact on life. Anything that lives here must be able to survive the heavy snows of winter as well as the rainless days of summer!

The trees that comprise this forest in the vicinity of Sequoia and Kings Canyon easily meet these conditions. The forest contains at least ten different species of evergreen trees, each requiring differing conditions for growth. Some prefer shade and others require strong sunlight; some need more water than others; some are more tolerant to cold. To make matters even more complicated, none of these trees grows in anything approaching a large, pure stand! This zone, therefore, is often described as a *mixed-conifer forest*; at least two or three trees of different species are usually present at any one location.

JOSEF MUENCH

Even without the giant sequoias, the world's
largest living things, the conifer forests of
the Sierra Nevada would be inhabited by giants.
The mild, wet winters and dry, warm summers
provide conditions optimum for the growth
of large, large trees. The giant sugar pines that grow
here (named for their sweet sap) are the
world's largest pines; even their pendulous cones
are huge—often eighteen inches long!

The most spectacular shared characteristic of these trees, however, is their great size. Sierran evergreens, almost without exception, grow far larger than conifers in other settings. The white and red firs grow to maximum heights of 150 to 200 feet and exceed basal diameters of five feet. Even the smallest conifers of the Sierra are huge when compared to those of other regions. Lodgepole pines, for instance, may grow up to eighty feet in height and two feet in diameter, far larger than most trees of this species growing in the Rocky Mountains.

The immensity of the giant sequoias—the largest measure thirty-five feet in basal diameter and up to three hundred feet in height—tends to overshadow other forest residents, however huge. Even the sugar pines don't seem particularly large in comparison, although the specimens seven feet in diameter and 180 feet tall that are common here are the largest of all the many pines to grow on the earth.

In the lowest and driest portions of the forest, yellow pine and incense cedar predominate. (Visitors often mistake the incense cedar for the sequoia because it bears a superficial resemblance to it.) These trees are more drought-tolerant than their neighbors and usually locate on south- and west-facing slopes.

White fir and sugar pine grow in the better-watered locations of the lower half of the forest (where the giant sequoia grows). Above 7,000 feet, white fir and yellow pine are gradually replaced by red fir and Jeffrey pine, respectively; and above 8,000 feet the western white pine replaces the sugar pine. Also growing at this elevation are juniper (in rocky, dry locations) and lodgepole (mainly along streams and in meadows).

Despite their many differences, these trees are alike in many ways: All are tall, narrow evergreens with drooping branches and small, needle-like leaves that they retain throughout the winter so that they can collect sunlight in the clear intervals between storms. The shapes of trees and needles allow them to shed snow easily and prevent ice buildup, the weight of which could pull the needles from the tree. Needles also conserve moisture, minimizing water loss during the coldest winter weather (when frozen soils block absorption through the roots) and the driest summer days.

GLENN VAN NIMWEGEN

The golden-mantled ground squirrel
enlivens the floor of the Sierran forests
on his frantic, scurrying searches for food.
Despite his stripes, he is not a chipmunk!

Open meadows, such as Log Meadow
in the Giant Forest, provide welcome, sunny
spaces in the dense sequoia forests. In
midsummer these swampy areas
become gardens of bright wildflowers.

*The timid-looking pine marten
is a voracious predator that
controls small-mammal populations.*

*The gentle forms of a mule deer and her fawn
add a note of serenity to a forest meadow.*

DAVID MUENCH

People often confuse the coast redwood (above) with the giant sequoia (sometimes called "Sierra redwood"). Both are sequoias; however, the giant sequoia (Sequoiadendron giganteum) grows only on the western slope of the Sierra Nevada, and the coast redwood (Sequoia sempervirons) prefers the coastal climate of northern California. The cinnamon-colored bark of the giant sequoia is pithy and spongy; the bark of the coast redwood is less distinctive and not very red (its name comes from the color of its heartwood). The coast redwood grows taller than any tree on earth, but the giant sequoia grows larger around. Thus, by virtue of sheer volume, the giant sequoia is the largest of all living things on this planet. Another important difference: Although their heartwoods are similar in color, that of the coast redwood is supple while that of the mature giant sequoia is weak and brittle. All commercial redwood lumber sold today comes from the coast redwood.

THE CRADLE OF GIANTS

The answer to the giantism found among the mountain conifers of the Sierra Nevada lies mainly in the mild climate here, the characteristic that distinguishes the Sierran snow forest from most other mountain forests. Even during the coldest weather, daytime temperatures seldom remain below freezing, and a long summer growing season allows tree growth in the Sierra to proceed at a much more rapid pace than is typical elsewhere.

No trees anywhere on earth grow larger than the giant sequoias (*Sequoiadendron giganteum*) of the Sierra Nevada. Of these, the General Sherman, Lincoln, and Washington trees (of Sequoia National Park) and the General Grant (of Kings Canyon National Park) are easily among the largest. The General Sherman is the *largest living thing on this planet*, with a maximum basal diameter of 36 feet and a height of 275 feet. Sizes are computed on the basis of volume, and the General Sherman has a total trunk volume of over 50,000 cubic feet. (Sequoias of equal height but with bases of between 15 and 25 feet are common in all the larger groves.)

The great girth of the giant sequoia gives it a clear edge in size over the coast redwood, also a species of sequoia, which usually grows *taller*. (The tallest standing giant sequoia is 311 feet tall; the tallest redwood, 367 feet.) Conversely, the tule

Several giant sequoias approach the General Sherman tree in total wood volume, but none matches or exceeds it. Recent measurements suggest that this monarch may be the fastest-growing as well as the largest of all living organisms.

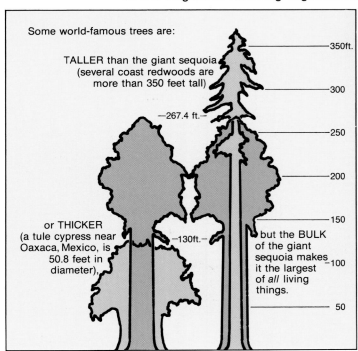

Some world-famous trees are:

TALLER than the giant sequoia (several coast redwoods are more than 350 feet tall)

—267.4 ft.—

or THICKER (a tule cypress near Oaxaca, Mexico, is 50.8 feet in diameter),

—130ft.—

but the BULK of the giant sequoia makes it the largest of *all* living things.

—350ft.
—300
—250
—200
—150
—100
—50

DICK DIETRICH

Sequoias grow so large simply because they live so long. All trees continue to grow as long as they live, and since sequoias grow fast and have huge life spans (perhaps thousands of years), they often reach gargantuan proportions. As a giant sequoia enters old age, it may start to lean, the result of erosion, fire damage, or root fungus.

In order to prosper in the Sierran snow forests, trees must be tall, narrow, and straight, with small, flexible branches. Here they rise like arrows into the blue Sierran sky, creating a pattern that is a study in strength and delicacy, height and breadth, color and form.

Sequoias have surprisingly shallow root systems, but they are extensive. Although the roots usually reach no deeper than five feet below ground, some may grow horizontally to more than a hundred feet in length!

ED COOPER

cypress grows much *broader* than the giant sequoia, but is not nearly as tall. The immensity of the giant sequoia is not usually comprehended by just looking at it, however. That is why the hollowed-out trunk that served as a cabin ("Tharp's Log"), the drive-through trunk, and other well-known oddities are so irresistible to people; comparison with familiar objects allows a better conceptual grasp of the true gigantism of this tree.

Many park visitors assume that, because the giant sequoia is so huge, it is a unique organism and thus is totally unlike any of its neighbors. Actually, the sequoia shares many characteristics with other forest residents; it is simply much, much larger! The giant sequoia is the culminating example of the regal inhabitants of the snow forest of the Sierra Nevada.

Since the end of the Ice Age, the giant sequoia has grown *naturally* only in the central and southern Sierra. Fossils of similar trees killed by changing climates have been found across much of western North America, but the range of the *living* tree is limited to approximately 75 small groves

found within a 260-mile stretch of the Sierra Nevada, a grove being defined as an area populated with sequoias—even as few as three—and surrounded by forests where they do not occur. The size of a grove depends upon how well the sequoia reproduces within that area.

The largest of these groves and the largest individual sequoias are found within Sequoia and Kings Canyon. These two national parks contain roughly thirty groves. (Yosemite National Park has three, and the remaining groves lie outside park boundaries, mainly in areas administered by the U.S. Forest Service.)

The fact that the giant sequoia is able to survive in only a small number of narrowly defined locations suggests that these trees have very special needs that are satisfied only by the environment of the Sierra, and even there the tree's range is limited. At elevations above 7,500 feet, for instance, cold temperatures and a short growing season usually preclude successful sequoia germination and growth. Prolonged below-zero weather can kill sequoias; and in areas where the snow-pack lasts into June or July, the growing season is

just too short for this sun-loving tree. (The few sequoias that do grow this high almost always grow on warm, south-facing slopes.)

Water availability also critically affects the sequoia. At the end of its first summer of growth, a seedling sequoia may have roots no longer than a foot. If, during the driest part of summer, this tiny tree does not have adequate soil moisture to tap within its shallow root range, it will die. Most seedling sequoias do perish in just this fashion. The locations in which the seventy-five groves exist evidently provide the stringent conditions required for sequoia growth—abundant soil moisture and a long growing season.

Over the hundreds of thousands of years the sequoia has existed as a species, it has had to make changes in order to survive. The most important of these adaptations have to do with fire, since lightning storms are common in the forest zone, even more so than in the foothills, and—like the foothills—the forest is highly flammable, at least toward summer's end.

Prior to the arrival of western man, lightning fires burned in most sequoia groves several times per century and sometimes as often as every ten years. Obviously, then, fire has been a major factor throughout the evolution of Sierran forests. In other words, any species that has survived to the present has had to learn to cope with fire.

The giant sequoia possesses several physical defenses that assist it in meeting this challenge. Foremost among these is its thick, fire-resistant bark, which usually burns poorly and also protects the tree from the intense, killing heat generated by fires, often more damaging to the tree than fire itself. The fibrous bark that clads the base of a giant sequoia may be over 18 inches thick, a more-than-adequate defense, although a particularly hot fire may succeed in burning into the wood, which *does* burn, although not as readily as some other Sierran conifer woods.

Given the great antiquity of the giant sequoia and the frequency of fires, it's not hard to understand why so many of these trees exhibit burn scars. A healing process is continually going on, however. New bark creeps over even the deepest "wound" at the rate of up to half an inch per year, until the breach is covered and the tree is once again fully protected. Often a tree will continue to grow even after fire has hollowed it out to the point that one can stand inside and look out its top at the sky.

FIRE: FOE—OR FRIEND?

Not only has the sequoia adapted in order to survive fires, it has learned—like the lowly chaparral of the foothills—to take *advantage* of them. Sequoia seedlings need more than moisture and mild temperatures; they need sunlight and access to bare, mineral soil. Fires provide these conditions by eliminating competing trees and burning off the undergrowth.

In order to fully utilize fire as a tool, the sequoia has developed a pattern of seed distribution that responds to the fire cycle: Whereas most trees in the conifer forest of the Sierra Nevada distribute their seeds as soon as they mature (usually at the end of the second summer of cone growth), the sequoia *retains* its seeds; the mature cones remain closed and on the tree. Each year additional cones are produced, so that eventually the number of seeds held on a single tree may be enormous. (A large sequoia may bear 40,000 cones, each containing one- to three-hundred seeds— seeds so small that it takes over 91,000 to weigh a pound.)

The reason for this mysterious behavior becomes apparent when fire sweeps through the forest. Most natural fires in the Sierra Nevada are ground fires, burning mainly in the understory of the forest. The fires produce large updrafts; and as

Repeated natural fires have damaged nearly all giant sequoias. But the fires themselves provide optimum conditions for germination. Hot updrafts dry and open old cones, thereby releasing seeds, which shower onto the forest floor. The freshly burned floor, now cleared of undergrowth and competing trees, allows the sequoia seedlings access to sunlight and soil minerals.

NPS PHOTO BY JOHN PALMER

this hot, dry air moves up through the foliage of the tree, it causes many of the old cones to dry and open. The sequoia has held its seed back for many years, awaiting the most productive moment. Now that moment has arrived, and the tree responds: Within a week or two after a fire, seeds begin to rain onto the freshly burned forest floor.

Sequoia germination is most successful on burned tracts in the spring following a summer or fall fire. Seedling mortality is high in a fire, but the number of germinations it prompts more than makes up for the losses. And because individual specimens have such a long life span, it is not necessary for sequoias to be prolific. In fact, if each mature sequoia produces only one successful offspring during the parent tree's several thousand years of life, the number of sequoias will remain constant!

THE WILL TO SURVIVE

Other factors help the sequoia to prosper in its chosen environment. Squirrels and beetles of certain species attack mature cones, unwittingly but effectively disseminating seeds in the intervals between fires and thereby giving the tree a backup seed-distribution method. Most important of these agents is the chickaree, whom we have already met. He relishes the fleshy scales of the cone but ignores the seeds. (It is known that a single chickaree can cut 10,000 cones in one season.) While he feasts, seeds are scattered over the forest floor.

The mild temperatures and abundant moisture that provide the basis for the existence of the great conifer forest also provide an excellent habitat for fungi. To discourage fungus growth, the mature sequoia has developed internal chemical

The chickaree acts as a distributor of sequoia seeds, which scatter to the ground as he relishes the fleshy scales of the small, woody sequoia cones.

Fire damage may weaken and thus threaten individual trees, but most giant sequoias can tolerate even such huge scars as this one, on the General Grant tree.

Western tanager

compounds, to a degree far surpassing most of its neighbors. These compounds make the tree unpalatable to fungi—and also to insects. Thus large sequoias are highly resistant to the ravages of insects even though more than a hundred species are known to inhabit them.

Next to its great size, the most amazing thing about the sequoia is its long life span. It seems incredible that a tree whose systems are so tenuously balanced with its chosen environment matures into an organism so well adapted that individual species have survived for two or three thousand years, some even longer. (Several western trees, including the western juniper and foxtail and limber pines live as long as the sequoia, and bristlecone pines live considerably longer.)

But the sequoia, once it has passed the seedling stage, is a very hardy tree whose wood is highly resistant to decay. It is also one of the fastest-growing in the world, a fact about this much publicized tree that is not so well known. It grows upward one to two feet per year until it is between two and three hundred feet high, and then (like people!) its growth is outward. The sequoia adds to its girth four- to six-hundredths of an inch of radial growth each year. Spread over such a massive body as the sequoia presents, this additional bulk can be compared roughly to that of a tree sixty feet tall and a foot and a half thick.

Finally, like all trees, the sequoia continues to grow as long as it lives; the older a sequoia is, the larger it is. Put simply, great age results in great size, and the remarkable sequoia is the ultimate example of the giantism found among the trees of the remarkable conifer forest of the Sierra Nevada.

A New Danger—Man

One of the factors that has inadvertently, and fortunately, served to save the sequoia is that, unlike the strong heartwood of the coast redwood,

the wood of the mature giant sequoia is weak and brittle—somewhat similar to balsa—and is therefore commercially undesirable. This isn't to say that people didn't *try* to make it pay, and in the early days—from the 1860s to the 1890s, when lumber companies were dazzled by thoughts of the huge number of board feet represented by each tree of this newly discovered species—mills, flumes, and camps sprang up in the forests. Ironically, the wood of this noble giant ended up being used for a lot of *little* things: shakes, railroad ties, fence posts, and grape stakes—sometimes produced right on the site—and cigar boxes.

But it often took a week or two for a team of four lumberjacks struggling with axes and crosscut saws to topple a particularly large sequoia. Moreover, when with a thunderous echo it finally crashed to the ground, most of the trunk was often shattered and worthless. Even the logs that remained intact and sound were just too huge to handle efficiently and economically.

By about 1910–15, the inaccessibility of the trees and the unprofitability of the wood had finally put an end to the harvesting of the sequoia in lands outside the already protected parks. In fact, two-thirds of the original, virgin stands are still intact. In contrast, more than ninety percent of the virgin stands of the coast redwood has been or is being *cut*. Perhaps having a wood that is not so desirable to man is, after all, the sequoia's "cleverest" protective device in its ongoing struggle for survival.

Shattered by lightning, scarred and gutted by fire, infested by insects and fungi, and hacked at by man, the giant sequoia lives on. Even when it finally topples (perhaps in a windstorm), it refuses to decay; and the sawdust lying in piles near trees logged more than eighty years ago still looks pink and fresh.

Perhaps, after all, the most amazing thing about the giant sequoia is neither its gargantuan girth nor its antiquity, but its indomitable will to survive in the face of incredible odds.

Forest Wildlife

The wildlife of the forest, like its trees, has adapted to the seasonal cycle that prevails here. Again, winter with its deep snow presents the greatest challenge. To understand what life is like for these creatures, one must know something about how they respond to the winters here.

Small, ground-dwelling rodents are common in the forest. Ground squirrels, mice, wood rats, moles, gophers, voles, and the like form the largest segment of the mammal population. Obviously, deep snow severely hampers the ability of these creatures to obtain food, and some must even go without. For many, this means hibernation; by lowering their levels of metabolism to the absolute minimum while lying dormant, these small creatures are able to last out the long winter. Only the gopher and the mole, living in the soil beneath the snow, and the mouse remain active throughout the winter.

The mule deer, larger and more mobile, chooses instead to escape the snow and cold; late in the fall, as the first snows arrive, it migrates toward the snow-free foothill zone. Many birds also migrate at this time: The ruby-crowned kinglet abandons its summer habitat in the red-fir forest and flies to a carefree winter in the foothills. The black-chinned hummingbird, however, prefers to winter in Mexico!

The chickaree remains active during the winter simply because he is a *tree* squirrel rather than a *ground* squirrel. His presence the year around entices several predators to remain also. Of these, the most visible are the coyote and the pine marten. The latter is particularly well equipped for life in the deep snow; during the winter months the pine marten grows long hair on its feet, enabling it to pass over even the softest powder snow with relative ease.

The great conifer forest of the Sierra Nevada is a world in which one can easily linger for many long, peaceful hours, while long-mired imaginations are revived, refreshed, and inspired.

The giant sequoias are, of course, the star performers of this realm. But they are eminently approachable: In spite of their massiveness, they have a friendly—even a gentle—quality, and the warm, wavy, spongy bark invites the familiarity of touching. Soon we realize we are seeing the sequoias as individuals, with recognizable features. Apparently others have felt the same; why else would so many of these giants bear personal labels—names that belong, moreover, to some of America's most admired heroes?

These tree-individuals grow here and there throughout the forest, and it crosses our minds, in this whimsical mood, that each has chosen for itself the spot in which it will grow and the companions with which it will spend its days.

Now the mist rolls in, intensifying the impression of utter enchantment, and it takes an almost physical effort to leave this fascinating world "peopled" by benign giants. But sounding down through the trees comes an invitation that must be heeded—and that is the siren call of the High Sierra.

STEPHEN J. KRASEMANN/DRK PHOTO

Steller's jay

DAVID MUENCH

Snow plant

LARRY BURTON

Yellow monkey flower

Overleaf: The Giant Forest of Sequoia National Park is unmatched for the quality of its sequoias, such as these in the Senate Group. Photo by Dick Dietrich

THE CANYONS OF THE KINGS RIVER

The Spaniards named it El Rio de los Santos Reyes, "The River of the Holy Kings," but little did they know of the river's origins high within the Sierra Nevada. The great twin canyons of the South and Middle forks of the Kings River, ranging from 4,000 to almost 8,000 feet in depth, dominate Kings Canyon National Park and furrow the already rugged Sierra with their fantastic forms. To travel through these rock-lined recesses is to explore some of the roughest terrain in North America. Only the canyon of the South Fork is easily accessible, even today. This gigantic canyon in its lower reaches is a narrow, water-filled gorge closely shadowed by walls of granite and marble. Above 4,000 feet, its character changes suddenly and drastically into that of a cliff-dominated but flat-floored glacial valley. Beautiful as this gentle valley is, it is soon forgotten as one ascends into the great mazes of alpine gorges and ridges that constitute the rugged climax of the Sierra.

Spring in South Fork Canyon introduces drama of
almost indescribable impact as the wild river,
swollen by snow melt, rushes through rocky gorges
and hurls white water against dark canyon walls.
The South Fork of the Kings River descends
through its steep canyons at a rate several times
faster than that of the Colorado River as it passes
through Grand Canyon. To stand on the banks
of this raging river is to confront firsthand the
awesome power of nature unrestrained. In contrast,
the springs and moss-covered rocks of the upper
canyon are a study in tranquility.

The daily habitat of the mountain lion is the rugged Kings River Sierra country, an area that intimidates all but the most determined of hikers. The canyons support an abundant variety of wildlife, including the deer, who grazes portions of the canyons throughout the year and, inevitably, is pursued by the mountain lion.

ERWIN & PEGGY BAUER

The incredible power that glacial erosion can exert does not become fully evident until one reaches "The Sphinx," several miles upstream of Cedar Grove. During the Ice Age, several thousand feet of moving ice filled and shaped these gorges.

The sylvan tranquility of Zumwalt Meadow contrasts strongly with the dramatic chaos of surrounding walls and canyons. Here, in the heart of the rough canyon country, lies Kings Canyon a nearly flat-floored valley about a half-mile wide and six miles long.

KENT & DONNA DANNEN

JOSEF MUENCH

*Within these colossal canyons
we feel tiny, insignificant.
Our place here is not to change and
not to dominate, but only to enjoy.*

JEFF GNASS

DAVID MUENCH

Those who spend the time to explore Kings Canyon slowly and thoroughly will reap dividends far exceeding the investment. The canyon has endless scenes to savor and memorize— from minute details, such as the bright accents blue lupine makes against rushing water, to immense panoramas, such as sun-tinged or blue-silhouetted canyon walls. Were there no giant sequoia, no High Sierra, there would still have to be a Kings Canyon National Park.

The High Country

The August sun that promises such heat in the foothills and touches the forest so gently seems almost cold as it rises grandly above the forbidding wall of granite peaks that comprise the Sierra Crest. It is the warmest month of the year, yet the small patches of grass that we see here and there along the rocky shore of a mountain lake are covered with frost. In this world that lies above 9,000 feet, the southern Sierra takes on a radically different character.

Life is sparse here, and stunted; avalanches and cold have seen to that. The four gnarled foxtail pines that stand like lonely sentinels near the glacial lake are the only *large* plants within a half

Life above 9,000 feet takes on forms far different from those of the lower slopes. Shaped by the harsh environment here, the stark trunks of foxtail pines reach out with gnarled fingers from a rockbound birthplace.

John Muir summed it up a century ago when he described the Sierra Nevada as the "range of light." In the crystal clarity of the High Sierra, human senses are sharpened by the interaction of rock, water, sun, and blue, blue sky.

Despite the severity of the high country, life is present and even occasionally abundant. Animals such as the yellow-bellied marmot thrive in settings that offer little or no physical comfort for man.

Clark's nutcracker

Buttercup

Each creature that inhabits the alpine zone of the Sierra must negotiate a separate peace with the harsh surroundings. The tiny, fragile pika survives in large numbers here because in the autumn it stores grasses to feed upon during the long winter.

mile to survive the onslaught of these relentless forces.

As the morning shadows recede, the dark-blue contours of the lake become visible. A half-mile long and carved almost entirely from granite, the lake lies at 11,000 feet and is closely surrounded by ridges that soar upward for another two thousand feet. The south shore lies partially buried in a mass of mixed rock and ice ten feet deep, a scene that is an eloquent reminder of the fury of last winter's avalanches.

On the sunny, northern side of the lake, near the four pines, a pika scurries from rock to rock, fearful of the dangers the open sky might hold. Stopping at a patch of yellow-green bunchgrass, the small, hampster-like creature sets to work.

When he has cut thirty or forty grass stems off near the ground, he gathers them into a bundle and, grasping them in his tiny mouth, carries them to the shelter of a protruding rock near his den, where he carefully arranges the cut grass to dry. Then back again for more. The pika is preparing his winter food supply.

Watching all this activity from the largest pine, the Clark's nutcracker—a black-and-white bird as large as a crow—takes a break from his own work, then resumes his leisurely task of dismantling a pine cone, extracting and eating the seeds. Below, in the shallow water near the edge of the lake, a yellow-legged frog basks, waiting for the morning sun to entice to the surface the many small insects that will constitute his lunch.

AN ARCTIC CLIMATE

This land of rock, light, water, and few living things is the true "high country" of the Sierra Nevada. This type of terrain makes up about half of Sequoia National Park and at least three-quarters of Kings Canyon National Park.

The climate here contrasts starkly with that of lowland California. It is literally an *arctic* climate and thus is more comparable to the climate of northern Alaska. In this winter-dominated land, summer is only a brief interruption followed closely by mid-September frosts, which nightly silver most of the high country, and October snows, which cloak the shady northern and eastern slopes. The six months of true winter have begun by November, and freezing weather is the norm; temperatures often plunge well below zero at night and rarely climb above the thirties during the day.

The winter storm cycles that buffet the foothills and forest also lash the high country, but their effects here are far more severe. Windblown, granular snow sweeps across bare, open surfaces, abrading the few living things that lie in its path.

The crest of the Sierra Nevada forms the eastern boundary of both Sequoia and Kings Canyon national parks. Studded with peaks 13,000 and even 14,000 feet high, the crest is one of the great natural barriers of North America. No road crosses the Sierra within these two parks, and it is easy to see why!
Huge glaciers were born here in times past, and small ones remain today. Ice and snow are a permanent part of this arctic environment. Can one imagine the High Sierra any other way?

WILLIAM C. TWEED

During the heart of winter, the snowpack builds steadily on all but a few south-facing slopes, and snow drifts to depths of fifteen to twenty feet. By February, a blanket of snow and ice covers all but the very largest promontories, and even those are ice-glazed.

Winter avalanches devastate the already barren alpine slopes after most storms, scouring the land with savage intensity, uprooting valiant pioneering seedlings and carrying great quantities of rock along their icy courses. On some slopes the avalanches are so persistent and abrasive that they actually shape the surface of the mountain, grinding out smooth, steep chutes.

Despite their severity, the snows of modern times are only a faint imitation of those of times past. Over much of the last three million years, the high country was buried beneath a permanent layer of ice—the glaciers of the Ice Age. These relentlessly moving ice sheets shaped the land and determined its character: They removed soils, leaving only polished rock behind; they widened and sometimes deepened canyons; they sculpted the very peaks themselves. The last of the large Sierra glaciers melted about ten thousand years ago. Today Sequoia and Kings Canyon contain only small glaciers, but these remnants serve to remind us of the great power exerted by their predecessors.

By May, winter finally, almost abruptly, has

GALEN ROWELL

Mount Goddard on the east ridge of Evolution Basin is surrounded by many glacial lakes. Such lakes decorate the high country in countless numbers.

relaxed its frigid grip. Perhaps, like the foothills, the high country has only two seasons. By June, warm weather has already invaded the High Sierra, and the snow melts rapidly on all but the most shaded of exposures.

July and August constitute the short, true summer, a season typified by clear skies and warm days. At the 10,000-foot level, temperatures range from the thirties to the sixties. Days often *feel* much warmer, however, because of the lack of filtering material in the atmosphere between the sun and these high elevations. The high country receives *more* radiant heat from the sun while having *less* heat in the air than lower elevations. Winter travelers notice this same phenomenon: Radiant heat may make a skier uncomfortably warm on a clear windless, 35° day!

August has not yet drawn to a close when the weather begins to cool again, a trend that continues gently but noticeably throughout September and October. Dryness still prevails during that period, but by November the snows have returned and the cycle has been completed once again.

SURVIVAL ON THE HEIGHTS

Life occurs, however sparsely, in every part of this rocky country. Few trees live above 11,000 feet, but grasses, flowers, lichens—even birds and small mammals—inhabit the slopes up to and including the summits of the highest peaks, some of which exceed 14,000 feet.

The harsh environment does not, of course, allow life to exist in the same forms it exhibits at lower elevations, and the changes are particularly obvious in plants. The trees of the high country, for example, bear little resemblance to their neighbors in the great forest below. As we proceed upslope, the trees become progressively smaller. The lodgepole pine is a dramatic example: Whereas at 9,000 feet this tree was erect and tall, at 11,000 feet it is a ground-hugging shrub. Only the foxtail pine seems able to maintain its erect nature at timberline. Largeness, much less giantism, is unknown in this alpine land; indeed, the short growing season so limits growth that a tree fifty feet tall and three or four feet at its base *is* a giant here.

The low profile of alpine plants allows them

DAVID MUENCH

The beauty of the High Sierra is more than breathtaking vistas. These panoramas may demand complete absorption at first, but as one travels this wonderful region, attention increasingly turns to such delightful details as the flowers and ferns that hide among jumbled rocks in a bright cascade that flows beside a high-country trail.

47

The bighorn sheep, once common throughout the Sierra, now inhabits Sequoia and Kings Canyon in remnant populations only.

to take full advantage of the warmer temperatures that prevail in the soil and the air immediately above it. Temperatures drop drastically only a few feet above the ground. (This temperature reading, taken at New Army Pass in Sequoia National Park, is typical: At 1:00 p.m., on a cloudless day, the surface temperature was 65° F.; at five feet above ground, the air temperature was 42°!) On the highest ridges, few plants grow more than two inches tall.

There is little danger of forest fire here. The trees of the high country grow either alone or in open, scattered stands; when lightning strikes a tree, it usually burns only that particular one. Thus the high-country trees, unlike their relatives downslope, have little incentive to develop fire-protection measures, and highly flammable pitch is present in copious amounts.

Many high-country plants counteract the dryness here with water-conserving features such as the short, thick needles of timberline trees and the thick leaves of many alpine wildflowers. Alpine plants often display characteristics very similar to those of plants in the hot, sandy valley floor to the east. By late summer, much of the high country is indeed a high, cold *desert.*

Animal life here exists under the same severe constraints. Hibernation is the answer for many high-country residents, even more so than for forest animals. The yellow-bellied marmot, for example, often sleeps from October to May, becoming active only during the short summer months.

Considering winter's severity, a surprising number of high-country animals remain active throughout its long duration. The pika feeds on harvested grasses (but almost never pokes his head above the snow). Porcupines gnaw on tree trunks, eating the live tissue beneath the bark. The Clark's nutcracker and the mountain chickadee are in evidence the year around, as are predators such as the pine marten, red fox, and mountain coyote.

In recent years, another animal has appeared on the scene, and its impact upon this domain has been great. Man has always been lured by the high country, perhaps drawn not so much by a desire to learn about it as to exploit its resources and to experience the thrill of traversing the highest points that lay so challengingly within his view.

But whatever the reasons that first brought man here, the special character of the high country continues to exert an irresistible appeal. Today the High Sierra is crisscrossed by dozens of trails that provide an infinite variety of breathtaking vistas and intimate scenes. Perhaps the most lasting of these is the view *inward.* For to know something of the secrets of the High Sierra is to learn something of that mysterious and elusive thing that lies within us all and is called man's *soul.*

Why climb to the top? The question is as old as mountain-climbing itself, and the answers are as numerous as those who do it. The countless summits of the parks provide a rugged playground for those who seek the high places. Some peaks are easily accessible; Mount Whitney is one of these. Others present rigorous technical challenges that test the most experienced of climbers.

MINERAL KING

*Mineral King—named by optimistic miners who flocked into this alpine valley in the 1870s—
never produced much silver, but the excitement of the search did result in a lasting legacy:
the winding, twisting, hundred-year-old road that is the only road in the southern Sierra to
reach the actual edge of the high country. For nearly seventy years after the mines died,
Mineral King remained a quiet, summer-cabin community. All this changed in the 1960s,
when plans surfaced for a giant ski resort here. Feelings ran high between those who
supported massive development and those who felt the small valley was too fragile and too
special for such a destiny. In 1978, after a decade of controversy, Congress resolved the
issue by adding Mineral King to Sequoia National Park, thus ensuring the preservation of its
unique natural beauty for all time.*

Mineral Lakes basin is one of a number of lake chains that lie within the Mineral King addition area.

WILLIAM C. TWEED

Those Who
Came Before . . .

Just how long man has been a part of the Sierra Nevada environment is not known. Although man may have arrived in North America tens of thousands of years ago, the Sierra certainly has not been inhabited that long. We know that summer camps were regularly occupied about a thousand years ago, but these sites may have been used on occasion long before that.

Like other mammals, primitive man came to understand the different climates and seasons of the Sierra and to develop strategies by which he could take advantage of its great variety. These early peoples wintered in large encampments in the foothills, sustaining themselves mainly on the acorns produced by foothill oaks. (Hospital Rock in Sequoia National Park was the site of such a camp.) During the warm summer months, when the foothills became hot and inhospitable, the Indians moved to the forests and mountains. Arrowheads, obsidian chips, and other evidences reveal that they had many encampments throughout all of the Sequoia and Kings Canyon country.

Indian populations were relatively small, but food was abundant; so the Indians had only a minor impact on the natural systems of the area. These Indians consisted of four groups: the *Western Mono (Monache)* of the Kaweah and Kings area, the *Tubatulabal* of the Kern River area, the *Paiutes* of the Owens Valley east of the Sierra Crest, and the *Yokuts* of the San Joaquin Valley. The first three groups—all Shoshonean—had a great deal of contact with one another, and the Yokuts visited occasionally for purposes of trading and hunting, or just to get away from the valley heat.

Spanish explorers and missionaries who came to the California coast as early as 1542 were oblivious to the Sierra Nevada, and those who came into the San Joaquin Valley more than two centuries later did little more than view the snow-clad

DICK DIETRICH

mountains from afar. It was, however, Spaniards—the Moraga party—in search of a mission site who named Kings River (and eventually, by association, Kings Canyon), which they called "The River of the Holy Kings."

Other than a few visits by trappers, the area was still largely untraveled in 1848, when the United States acquired California from Mexico. Two years later, Lieutenant George H. Derby, U.S.A., conducted the first official survey of the San Joaquin Valley. The information offered by his rough map and sketchy report was of little value. (This same year did, however, see the establishment of the first permanent community in the area, near the present town of Visalia.) A second government survey led by Robert B. Williamson in 1853 likewise did little, except to describe the lower Kaweah River and the luxurious vegetation and rich soil of the area. It was enough, however, to whet appetites back East, and the settlers began to trickle in.

Indians were still living in the mountains when the first white settlers arrived in the 1850s, but the white man's diseases—smallpox, measles, and scarlet fever—proved so disastrous to them that by 1865 the Indians had largely vanished from the scene.

Ranchers and early settlers came into the region of Sequoia and Kings Canyon as cattle ranchers, lured by tales of the thick grasses of the foothills, which would provide excellent forage, and the mountain meadows of the forests, which would provide excellent late-summer grazing.

Many of these people had first come to California in the stampede following the discovery of gold there. One of the earliest was Hale D. Tharp, who came to the Placerville gold fields in 1852 but soon moved on to Tulare County to enter the cattle business. He is credited with having "discovered" the grove now known as the "Giant Forest," probably the most magnificent of the groves that contain the giant sequoia. Motivated by an interest in the Indians then living there, he explored the Giant Forest on an intimate basis. He established his claim to it by driving some of his horses to Log Meadow in 1861 and later pasturing his cattle there.

Tharp was not the first of the new wave, however, to discover the giant sequoias, in the early days often known simply as the "Big Trees." This distinction probably belongs to Lieutenant Joseph R. Walker, whose expedition in 1833 discovered—in addition to the Yosemite Valley—one

Hale Tharp, the first white man to visit the Giant Forest, built this shelter for himself out of a fallen, fire-hollowed sequoia log.

Cloud Canyon; the Whaleback. By the 1860s the lush high-country meadows had attracted the attention of California sheep ranchers in search of summer range. For over thirty years portions of the High Sierra were heavily grazed. Particularly hard hit was the area of the Kern River headwaters in Sequoia National Park.

WILLIAM C. TWEED

Lowland canyons served as highways for man in the Sierra.

ED COOPER

of the great sequoia stands of Yosemite. Later, in 1852, A. T. Dowd stumbled upon the Calaveras Grove while chasing a wounded bear, and it was this incident that sparked the spread of the news of the huge trees throughout the world.

In the intervening years other pioneers must have chanced upon similar groves or individual trees, but they either did not record their discoveries or people simply didn't believe them. Captain John J. Kuykendall and his party, probably the first white men to view Kings Canyon and the northern section of what is now Sequoia National Park, saw no sequoias. But they had been sent to subdue Indians reluctant to come in for treaty talks, and perhaps Indian-chasing took all their time and attention. (The groves do tend to be widely scattered, and small stands are often obscured by other trees.)

All the prospecting for precious minerals that went on in the area of the park yielded little, except for the Mineral King silver strike in 1873, which held the interest of seekers of riches until the boom ceased in 1881.

Meanwhile, sheepherders had discovered the ideal climate and free mountain pastures that made certain areas of the park—particularly the upper Kings and Kern rivers—a paradise for sheepmen. Most of the sheep flocks were tended by French and Spanish Basques who performed their lonely tasks for a nominal wage paid by American employers.

It was inevitable that the giant sequoia of the Sierra Nevada would be sought out by lumbermen. So it was that, by the turn of the century, large-scale sequoia logging was underway in many groves. Fortunately, the brittle wood turned out to be commercially undesirable, and logging was discontinued. Today, the stumps and broken logs left behind by early loggers are surrounded, usually, by seedling sequoia forests.

Over the years, sheepherding had a disastrous effect on the land, including the destruction of precious mountain watersheds: Overgrazing was a constant practice, due to the lack of any controls over use of the land; and the sharp hooves of the sheep cut harmfully into the fragile alpine meadows upslope.

It was inevitable that the discovery and subsequent publicizing of the giant sequoia would attract the attention of lumbermen. Logging operations began soon after settlers appeared in the treeless San Joaquin Valley and looked to the lower fringe of the conifer forest as a nearby source of lumber for their buildings. By the 1870s lumbermen had invaded the forests of the southern Sierra. The practice was to set up small mills right in the timber (such as the mills near Big Stump Basin) and to manufacture fence posts and the like on the spot. This eliminated the necessity for transporting the huge logs for long distances.

Most of the trees felled were pine and fir. The wood of the mature sequoia was weak and brittle, but it was a common practice to cut some of the largest sequoias and send them to the East for exhibition—the fate of the Centennial, Mark Twain, and General Noble trees. Perhaps this was the only method by which eastern skeptics could be convinced. Even a sequoia cross-section twenty feet wide that had been cut and shipped had not been sufficient evidence; it had been labeled the "California hoax" by unbelieving Easterners.

Logging of the sequoia picked up, however, especially after 1889 when the Sanger Lumber Company constructed a fifty-mile-long flume that could transport lumber from the rugged timberlands to the San Joaquin Valley. This single flume is said to have been responsible for the destruction of one of the finest stands of giant sequoias in existence, present at one time in Converse Basin.

A NEW ISSUE: CONSERVATION

Amidst this exploitation, which threatened to envelop the Sierra on a wholesale scale, a few voices of protest began to be heard. John Muir first visited the southern Sierra in 1873, exploring the Grant Grove and Kings Canyon areas, and returned two years later to explore (and name) the Giant Forest. His writings in the cause of conservation are numerous and well known; of the cutting of the magnificent sequoias, he said *"As well sell the rain clouds and the snow and the rivers to be cut up and carried away, if that were possible."*

Previous to this time, in 1864, a California Geological Survey party led by William H. Brewer entered and explored the heretofore unknown country of the High Sierra. They stood on the crest and looked down into the spectacular country that lay below and to each side, probably the first time white men had been in this exalted region. This exploration was actually little more than a reconnaissance, but it did serve to pinpoint the major features of the range. (Two members of this party went on to explore the highest of these peaks and to name the tallest of them "Mount Whitney" in honor of the survey's director.) And it made known for the first time the scenic, rugged nature of the southern Sierra.

Perhaps spurred by sentiments such as Muir's and the descriptions of the Brewer party and other explorations that followed it, a movement began to develop in the San Joaquin Valley in the 1880s to preserve certain tracts of the Sierra.

The movement had two main bases of support: farmers who realized that destruction of mountain vegetation was disturbing stream flow and irrigation, and a small group of men who wanted to save at least a few groves of the giant sequoia. These two groups coalesced under the leadership of George Stewart, editor of the *Visalia Delta* in the San Joaquin Valley. Stewart's determined editorials called for congressional action.

The efforts of these groups were rewarded in September, 1890, when an act of Congress signed by President Benjamin Harrison created "Sequoia National Park." Less than one week later a second act tripled the size of Sequoia and also preserved Grant Grove by creating "General Grant National Park." The addition of the Grant Grove, and possibly the enlargement of Sequoia, was accomplished largely through the efforts of Daniel K. Zumwalt, of the Southern Pacific Railroad, who was no doubt aware of the economic benefits it would engender, including the attraction of many tourists to the area. Although some have ques-

The threatened logging of such giants as the McKinley tree prompted early park legislation.

tioned the motives involved in this maneuver, there is no doubt that the results were of ultimate benefit to everybody. Incidentally, these two parks were only the second and fourth national parks to be established in the United States. (Yellowstone was the first, and Yosemite—contained in the bill with General Grant National Park—was the third.)

News of the enlargement sparked a brief but intense protest by some members of the "Kaweah Colony," pioneering residents. They had supported the park's establishment but now felt their land claims were being endangered by the boundary enlargement. For the most part, however, the attitude of the residents was favorable. In fact, petitions were drawn up by San Joaquin Valley farmers to declare the remainder of the southern Sierra to be the "Sierra Forest Reserve." In 1893, President Benjamin Harrison signed into being this entity, which was the forerunner of several of today's national *forests*.

Early administration of the two national parks of the southern Sierra was haphazard at best. Illegal lumbering, grazing, and hunting continued to cause problems. The parks, under the administration of the War Department, were protected by cavalry troops during the summer months and were forgotten during the winters. In 1900, encouraged by the military superintendents of the park, the War Department brought in a civilian park ranger to provide year-round protection. In 1914 the War Department withdrew completely from the park and the Department of the Interior assumed full control. Walter Fry, who had been serving as a civilian park ranger (the second to so serve) became the first civilian superintendent of the park.

By the turn of the century the national parks and the forest reserves (national forests) had begun to move in separate directions. National parks were managed with the goal of preserving scenic and historic resources in as natural a condition as possible, while national forests were managed under what is now called the "multiple-use" doctrine, which permits hunting, logging, dam-building, etc., under controlled conditions. The conflict between these philosophies began to surface in the early 1920s, when a proposal to enlarge

Nature produced the giant sequoias, and man fortunately saw fit to protect them early on. Even at the time when resource exploitation was at its uncontrolled worst (the late nineteenth century), American citizens realized that these trees were too special to be destroyed.

K. C. DENDOOVEN

Physical development of Sequoia National Park peaked during the Great Depression, when the Civilian Conservation Corps (CCC) program put thousands of men to work in the park. Among the many reminders of this period in Sequoia National Park is the hand-carved sign at the southern entrance. The giant sequoia (and therefore the park) is said to have been named in honor of the "red man," specifically the great Cherokee leader Sequoyah, who invented an entire alphabet so that his people could learn to read and write.

Sequoia National Park was being considered.

Two national-forest areas adjacent to the existing parks attracted particular attention: the Kern Canyon area, which included the highest peaks in the Sierra Nevada, and the Kings River Canyon country north of Sequoia and east of General Grant, which contained a wonderland of high peaks as well as two canyons of Yosemite-like proportions. Conservationists, the Sierra Club in the forefront, wanted permanent preservation of these outstanding scenic areas and drove for their removal from the Sequoia National Forest. But they were seriously opposed in their Kings Canyon enlargement efforts by those who hoped to build reservoirs and power plants in the canyons. A resulting compromise led to the 1926 addition of the Kern area alone to Sequoia.

The Kings Canyon National Park idea refused to die, however, and renewed efforts paid off in 1940, when Kings Canyon National Park was signed into being by President Franklin D. Roosevelt. The old General Grant National Park became part of the newer and much larger unit. In 1943, as a wartime economy measure, Sequoia and Kings Canyon were merged under a single superintendent, an arrangement that proved so effective and practical that it has been continued to this day.

DAVID MUENCH

ing cause for conservationists. Campaigns to preserve this delicate region, led mainly by the Sierra Club, resulted in the addition of Mineral King to Sequoia National Park in 1978.

THE PARKS TODAY

Today, Sequoia and Kings Canyon National Parks receive well over 2 million visitors annually. They come to the parks to seek escape and respite from the cities of modern industrial America and from the heat of lowland California.

The three natural zones of the parks still affect human activity. Foothill use has been expanding, but it is still the giant sequoia groves in the great conifer forests that is the main attraction for visitors. Most of the lodges and campgrounds of the parks are within the area of the cool, green forests. Traditional recreational forest uses, including day-hiking, picnicking, and camping, are favorite pastimes in these areas.

As for the high country, a different management philosophy is in effect, in the hope of preserving the wilderness condition of the magnificent canyons and ridges of the High Sierra. A large, roadless area forms the heart of these two parks, and those who aim to know the parks intimately and thoroughly must become wilderness travelers. For these people, the Park Service maintains an extensive network of wilderness trails. Famous trails used by backpackers and stock parties include the John Muir and High Sierra trails.

Heavy visitation of the parks has caused problems for their administrators. For example, the natural tendency of visitors to congregate in the sequoia groves caused few difficulties when park visitation was relatively light, but today the presence of large numbers of people in these groves—together with the developments they require—roads, lodges, utility systems, and trails—has an undeniable impact on the natural environment. Soil erosion can result from heavy human use, and when shallow-rooted sequoias are present, such erosion can become serious. Human beings inevitably lessen the quality of air and

Between 1920 and 1940, while these enlargement campaigns were going on, the National Park Service was building or authorizing the construction of modern lodges, roads, and trails for the parks of the southern Sierra. These improvements, especially the construction of good roads, allowed park use to soar, and the number of visitors accelerated even faster after World War II.

MINERAL KING AND THE DISNEY CORPORATION

Controversy regarding potential enlargement returned to Sequoia and Kings Canyon again in the 1970s, when the U.S. Forest Service proposed development of a large ski resort at Mineral King, which essentially occupied a small pocket in the southern boundary of Sequoia National Park.

Since the silver rush to Mineral King had ended in the early 1880s, this spectacular mountain valley had received only minimal attention. The development proposals put forward by the Disney Corporation, in cooperation with the Forest Service, shattered the peace at Mineral King, however, and ultimately made the valley a rally-

Particularly dramatic has been the increase in back-country travel in recent decades. As late as the 1950s the High Sierra received only light use in most places. Today so many hikers and backpackers are seeking the freedom offered only by wilderness areas that their numbers must be controlled through the establishment of quotas and the use of permits.

Muir Pass hut

Granite blocks, east face of Mount Hale

water, and the presence of large numbers of buildings and cars can result in the creation of an unnatural, overly civilized atmosphere.

These problems are not new. Even before World War II, the Park Service began to question the wisdom of locating park facilities among the sequoias, and the past several decades have seen the removal of numerous park functions to less fragile locations. It is planned to continue this process until the largest sequoia groves, such as the Giant Forest, have been returned to as near a pristine state as possible.

The back country, too, has felt the impact of more and more people. It has become so popular and overcrowded with campers that parts of this wilderness have suffered much physical and esthetic damage. To alleviate the problem, the Park Service has implemented a wilderness-trail quota system, which limits the number of people who can visit certain popular areas and encourages use of lesser-known high-country areas.

JEFF GNASS

Fire management is another area of recent concern. For many years a policy of total suppression of all fires was followed in the parks, but as the natural role that fire plays in the systems of the Sierra became apparent, this traditional policy has been abandoned. Now, most natural fires above 8,000 feet are allowed to burn without interference. At lower altitudes, where large amounts of fuel have accumulated under the old no-fire philosophy, the Park Service now carries out prescribed burning under controlled conditions.

The granite massif of Mount Whitney stands guard over the eastern boundary of Sequoia and Kings Canyon. Looking at these rugged mountains from afar, it is easy to misjudge them as an indestructible part of the landscape. Although the mountains themselves are indeed massive and enduring, the variety of life they harbor is fragile and transitory.

SUGGESTED READING

SUGGESTED READING

ARNO, STEPHEN. *Discovering Sierra Trees.* Yosemite and Sequoia national parks: Yosemite and Sequoia natural history associations, 1973.

BASEY, HAROLD. *Discovering Sierra Reptiles and Amphibians.* Yosemite and Sequoia national parks: Yosemite and Sequoia natural history associations, 1976.

BEEDY, EDWARD C. and STEPHEN L. GRANHOLM. *Discovering Western Birds: Western Slope.* Yosemite and Sequoia national parks: Yosemite and Sequoia natural history associations, 1985.

DILSAVER, LARY and WILLIAM C. TWEED. *Challenge of the Big Trees: A Resource History of Sequoia and Kings Canyon National Parks.* Sequoia National Park: Sequoia Natural History Association, 1990.

GRATER, RUSSELL K. *Discovering Sierra Mammals.* Yosemite and Sequoia national parks: Yosemite and Sequoia natural history associations, 1978.

HARVEY, H. T.; H. S. SHELLHAMMER; and R. E. STECKER. *The Giant Sequoia.* Sequoia National Park: Sequoia Natural History Association, 1980.

PALMER, JOHN J. *in pictures SEQUOIA & KINGS CANYON The Continuing Story.* Las Vegas, Nevada: KC Publications, Inc., 1990.

TWEED, WILLIAM C. *Kaweah Remembered: The Story of the Kaweah Colony and the Founding of Sequoia National Park.* Sequoia National Park: Sequoia Natural History Association, 1986.

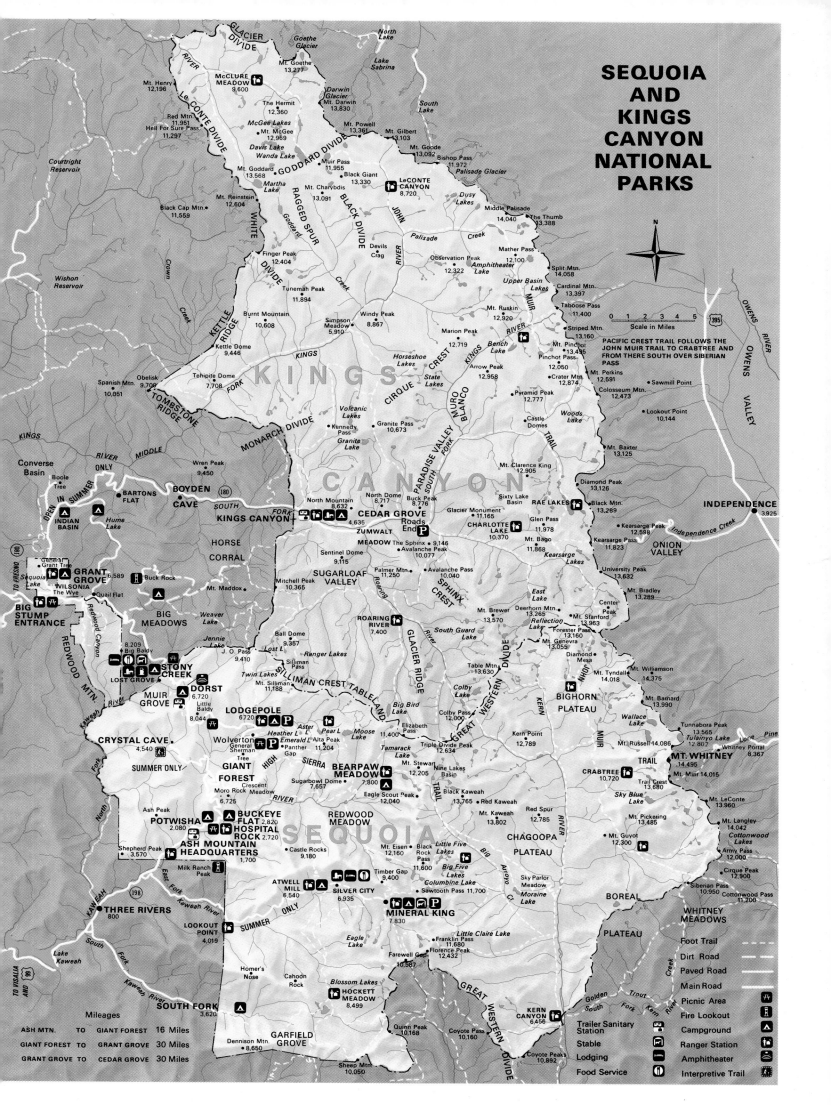

SEQUOIA AND KINGS CANYON NATIONAL PARKS

PACIFIC CREST TRAIL FOLLOWS THE JOHN MUIR TRAIL TO CRABTREE AND FROM THERE SOUTH OVER SIBERIAN PASS

Scale in Miles
0 1 2 3 4 5

Mileages

ASH MTN.	TO	GIANT FOREST	16 Miles
GIANT FOREST	TO	GRANT GROVE	30 Miles
GRANT GROVE	TO	CEDAR GROVE	30 Miles

Legend

- — — — Foot Trail
- ········· Dirt Road
- Paved Road
- Main Road
- Picnic Area
- Fire Lookout
- Campground
- Trailer Sanitary Station
- Ranger Station
- Stable
- Amphitheater
- Lodging
- Interpretive Trail
- Food Service

Centennial Parks

After a century of protection as national parks, Sequoia and Kings Canyon remain a land of striking natural variety—a land where enduring granite and fragile ecosystems co-exist. If judged against the century-old dreams of the founders, the parks are astounding successes; the Big Trees still stand and the web of life that surrounds them continues to prosper in the face of challenges that nineteenth century Americans never even imagined.

More than ever before, the parks are subject to what goes on around them. Ongoing research suggests that man-caused pollutants, especially ozone and acid precipitation, pose a very real threat to the ecosystems of the parks, and every year additional human development on surrounding lands makes the parks more isolated biologically.

Yet, if the parks are increasingly threatened by California's nearly thirty million residents, they are also more deeply loved and appreciated than ever before. Each year two million visitors stand beneath the ancient giants, and each one comes away changed in some way by their grandeur, and by their insistent reminder that the natural world is still the center of our human reality.

JOSEF MUENCH

Observed from Moro Rock, a winter sunset leaves the sequoia forest beached on a sea of clouds.

The giants of the sequoia forest emerge from the mists of the present as they have, in a larger sense, from the mists of the past.

Back cover: The High Sierra trail of Sequoia National Park winds its way though the incredible scenery of the Great Western Divide on the trail's seventy-mile route to the summit of Mount Whitney.

Photos by David Muench

Books in the Story Behind the Scenery series: Acadia, Alcatraz Island, Arches, Biscayne, Blue Ridge Parkway, Bryce Canyon, Canyon de Chelly, Canyonlands, Cape Cod, Capitol Reef, Channel Islands, Civil War Parks, Colonial, Crater Lake, Death Valley, Denali, Devils Tower, Dinosaur, Everglades, Fort Clatsop, Gettysburg, Glacier, Glen Canyon-Lake Powell, Grand Canyon, Grand Canyon-North Rim, Grand Teton, Great Basin, Great Smoky Mountains, Haleakala, Hawaii Volcanoes, Independence, Lake Mead-Hoover Dam, Lassen Volcanic, Lincoln Parks, Mammoth Cave, Mount Rainier, Mount Rushmore, Mount St. Helens, National Park Service, National Seashores, North Cascades, Olympic, Petrified Forest, Redwood, Rocky Mountain, Scotty's Castle, Sequoia & Kings Canyon, Shenandoah, Statue of Liberty, Theodore Roosevelt, Virgin Islands, Yellowstone, Yosemite, Zion.
NEW: in pictures—The Continuing Story: Bryce Canyon, Death Valley, Everglades, Glen Canyon-Lake Powell, Grand Canyon, Mount Rainier, Mount St. Helens, Petrified Forest, Sequoia & Kings Canyon, Yellowstone, Yosemite, Zion.

Published by KC Publications • Box 14429 • Las Vegas, NV 89114

Printed by Dong-A Printing and Publishing, Seoul, Korea
Color Separations by Kedia/Kwangyangsa Co., Ltd.